**TOMORROW
IS TOO LATE**

TOMORROW IS TOO LATE

Development and the environmental crisis in the Third World

FIDEL CASTRO

OCEAN

Cover photo by Osvaldo Salas
Cover design by David Spratt

ISBN paper 1-875284-73-7

First edition, 1993

Published by Ocean Press,
GPO Box 3279, Melbourne, Victoria 3001, Australia

Distributed in the USA by The Talman Company,
131 Spring Street, Suite 201E-N, New York, NY 10012, USA
Distributed in Britain and Europe by Central Books,
99 Wallis Road, London E9 5LN, Britain
Distributed in Southern Africa by Grassroots Books,
PO Box A267, Avondale, Harare, Zimbabwe
Distributed in Australia by Astam Books,
162-8 Parramatta Road, Stanmore, NSW 2048, Australia

Contents

Publisher's note

The gathering of world leaders at the Earth Summit in Rio de Janeiro in June 1992 was an opportunity for them to present their views on the global crisis. Some 107 heads of government or representatives spoke in succession.

Much of the world's media captured the political and philosophical dilemma facing the Summit by using the counterposed positions of the leaders of the United States and Cuba. New York's *Newsday* wrote: "By far the warmest reaction to the heads of state who spoke was for Cuban President Fidel Castro, who called for an end to 'selfishness' on the part of the industrialized world. In contrast, the reaction to President George Bush was cold, with only a smattering of applause as he refused to apologize for taking positions opposed by the rest of the world."

While Bush said he "did not come to Rio to apologize," Castro called for an end to the "selfishness, schemes of domination, insensitivity, irresponsibility and deceit" of the industrialized, consumer societies.

The speech of Cuban leader Fidel Castro — widely reported throughout the world — opens this book. It is followed by the full text of a document distributed to all delegates to the Earth Summit. Prepared by Castro, the document expands on the claim made in his address to the Summit that "the Third World cannot be blamed" for the threat posed to humankind by the "appalling destruction of the environment." His poignant call to arms concludes with the declaration that "tomorrow will be too late to do what should have been done a long time ago."

Development versus conservation of the environment: can the two be reconciled? Where does the responsibility for the destruction of the environment lie? Should the Third World and its expanding populations be held responsible for the crisis?

1

This document is a useful contribution to the international discussion on how to save and protect the resources of the planet, and perhaps our planet itself. It projects an unashamedly "Third World perspective" into the debate on both the causes and solutions to the crisis.

This book is published with the assistance of Editora Politica of Havana, Cuba. The cover photo and several of those included in this volume are by the late Osvaldo Salas, Cuba's foremost photographer.

CHAPTER 1

Humankind — an endangered species

An important biological species — humankind — is at risk of disappearing due to the rapid and progressive elimination of its natural habitat. We are becoming aware of this problem when it is almost too late to prevent it. It must be said that consumer societies are chiefly responsible for this appalling environmental destruction.

They were spawned by the former colonial metropolis. They are the off-spring of imperial policies which, in turn, brought forth the backwardness and poverty that have become the scourge of the great majority of humanity.

With only 20 percent of the world's population, they consume two-thirds of all metals and three-fourths of the energy produced worldwide. They have poisoned the seas and rivers. They have polluted the air. They have weakened and perforated the ozone layer. They have saturated the atmosphere with gases, altering climatic conditions with the catastrophic effects we are already beginning to suffer.

The forests are disappearing. The deserts are expanding. Billions of tons of fertile soil are washed every year into the sea. Numerous species are becoming extinct. Population pressures and poverty lead to desperate efforts to survive, even at the expense of nature. Third World countries, yesterday's colonies and today's nations exploited and plundered by an unjust economic order, cannot be blamed for all this.

The solution cannot be to prevent the development of those who need it the most. Because today, everything that contributes to underdevelopment and poverty is a flagrant rape of the environment.

As a result, tens of millions of men, women, and children die every year in the Third World, more than in each of the two world wars.

Unequal trade, protectionism and the foreign debt assault the ecological balance and promote the destruction of the environment. If we want to save humanity from this self-destruction, wealth and available technologies must be distributed better throughout the planet. Less luxury and less waste in a few countries would mean less poverty and hunger in much of the world.

Stop transferring to the Third World lifestyles and consumer habits that ruin the environment. Make human life more rational. Adopt a more just international economic order. Use science to achieve sustainable development without pollution. Pay the ecological debt instead of the foreign debt. Eradicate hunger and not humanity.

Now that the supposed threat of communism has disappeared and there is no more pretext to wage cold wars or continue the arms race and military spending, what then is preventing these resources from going immediately to promote Third World development and fight the ecological destruction threatening the planet?

Enough of selfishness. Enough of schemes of domination. Enough of insensitivity, irresponsibility and deceit. Tomorrow will be too late to do what we should have done a long time ago.

CHAPTER 2

The environmental crisis and the Third World

The significance of this meeting and the urgent need to make decisions on effective measures to protect humanity and ensure its very survival are lost on none of us who have come here to Rio de Janeiro in answer to the call to attend this Conference on the Environment and Development.

The accelerated and increasing deterioration of the environment is possibly the most serious long-term danger faced by the entire human species and in particular in what is still called the Third World. Alongside the ever-present risk of nuclear destruction, it is the worst threat ever faced by all of humanity. For underdeveloped countries, it is one of the most powerful factors worsening the living conditions of hundreds of millions of people in the Third World.

Never in the history of humanity has there been such a generalized and destructive aggression against all the planet's life systems. In the underdeveloped world, poverty and underdevelopment themselves are today the main factors multiplying the pressures imposed on the natural environment. The overexploitation of agricultural and pasture lands, inadequate agricultural methods, the lack of financial and technical resources all accumulate their noxious effects on the environment. Furthermore, in its zeal to obtain the largest possible profit margin, capitalist exploitation of natural resources and industrial capacities contributes its grave quota of destruction and adds new forms of pollution and degradation of the atmosphere. In the developed world, lifestyles that stimulate irrational consumerism and promote the waste and destruction of nonrenewable resources multiply the afflictions and tensions suffered by the local and global physical environment to unprecedented and heretofore unimaginable levels.

For the first time in its history, humanity is capable of altering the balance of the vital life systems and breaking the natural laws that govern evolution on the planet. It can destroy life in one fell swoop with a nuclear war. Through genetic engineering, it actively influences the accelerated mutation of species that needed millenia to consolidate naturally. For the first time, humanity is capable of changing the course of life.

It is already doing so by directly acting on the environment. The increasingly more obvious effects of humanity's irrational aggression towards the natural environment — which for opulent societies were until recently far-removed from their immediate preoccupations — are today not a mere distant threat, but a common reality for all nations.

That is why we are gathered here in Rio de Janeiro. Consciousness of the serious effects of environmental deterioration — although felt most directly, immediately and devastatingly by the poorest and most vulnerable part of the planet's population — has begun to spread beyond the geographical and social situation of the Third World to become a threat that affects all of humanity. Growing is the conviction that if humanity doesn't take the necessary steps in time, it could find itself facing the uncertain threshold of the destruction of all life on this planet.

Cuba, a small Third World country that is waging its battle to develop in the midst of singularly adverse circumstances, can nevertheless modestly offer to the world in general and the underdeveloped world in particular, its experience in conservation and protection of the environment. It also offers the results obtained by our people in diverse areas directly related to the issues that will be considered during this meeting's debates.

We take this opportunity to express our recognition to the government of our sister republic of Brazil and to its esteemed President Fernando Collor de Mello for the lofty task of hosting this conference, as well as our personal thanks for the amiable invitation for us to participate. I would like to make it clear that Cuba has come to this meeting with the decided will to contribute with all its might to achieving the goals that have brought us together, with the conviction that all the efforts we make in favor of these objectives is a concrete guarantee of our future.

The character and urgency of the ecological debate

Over the last two decades the issue of the environment has moved from the periphery to the very center of theoretical debates and decision-making processes in many parts of the world. In the extensive literature on ecological issues that has proliferated in our times, the internationalization of the debate on the environment and the ecological movement is often referred to as the outcome of a process of evolution of the last few years. One phenomenon that has had a determining effect on this consciousness-raising on a world level has been the emergence and activities of a growing number of nongovernmental environmental organizations, some of which are characterized by their militancy and the increasing spread of their influence.

At the root of this growing awareness has obviously been the fact that over the last 20 years the actual and potential effects of some of the global environmental problems that most worry humanity have become more evident. These include the deterioration of the ozone layer, global warming due to the so-called greenhouse effect, acid rain, other forms of environmental deterioration caused by the wasteful consumer model of the most developed countries, the loss of biological diversity, the pollution created by urban gigantism, the traffic across borders of dangerous waste, the pollution of underground and surface water reserves, of seas and coastal zones, deforestation, and the impoverishment of agricultural lands. Among all these very serious problems, one element that cannot help but be in the front line of the contemporary ecological debate is the awareness that, particularly in large sectors of the Third World where the immense majority of the population subsists in precarious conditions of poverty, the main endangered biological species is humanity itself.

Everyone knows that the last decade has been the hottest of the last hundred years, that it has included six of the seven hottest years known to humanity, and that the hottest year in recorded history was 1990. This global warming phenomenon, a consequence of what is called the "greenhouse effect," has important ecological, economic and social consequences. According to some estimates, if there is no limit put on present emissions of the gases that cause the greenhouse effect, the amount of carbon dioxide in the atmosphere will double between now and sometime between 2025 and 2050, causing an increase in average global temperature of between 1.5 and 4.5 degrees Celsius. An immediate effect of this phenomenon would be a rise in sea level of between 30 and 50 centimeters by the year 2050, and of about one meter by the year 2100, which would flood extensive continental coastal zones, some with high population density, and would affect a number of island states. Other forecasts are shorter term and more alarming.

Climatic transformations would, among other things, cause changes in rainfall and marine ecosystems, increasing the possibility of phenomena such as hurricanes, tropical cyclones and typhoons. Similarly, temperate zones would become more vulnerable to tropical diseases such as malaria, dengue and yellow fever and many of that area's crops would be severely affected, as in the case of wheat.

It has been calculated that the average global level of ozone in the stratosphere decreased by about five percent between 1979 and 1986. In the mid-1980s a hole was discovered in the ozone layer over the Antarctic, and, more recently, certain scientific reports state that the conditions exist for another to form over the Arctic circle. This exhaustion of the ozone layer increases the vulnerability of the planet's living beings to harmful ultraviolet rays and therefore carries with it enormous risks of a greater probability of illnesses such as skin cancer and eye disease, among others, as well as noticeable harm to livestock and certain crops.

The relative speed with which international negotiations have progressed, and with which concrete agreements have been adopted to reduce and eventually eliminate the use and production of chlorofluorocarbons and other gases harmful to the ozone layer, not only shows the developed countries' concern about the depletion of the ozone layer. It also shows the interest on the part of certain of these countries' economic circles to lead the way with the suggested technological transformations and control the transfer of this technology at the international level. It would be desirable to arrive at a similar collective position within this conference, for whatever reasons, that would allow us to take concrete and effective measures to confront other environmental situations that are as worrisome and more immediate than the deterioration of the ozone layer.

Between 1860 and 1985, emissions of sulphur dioxide, one of the main causes of acid rain, increased from seven million to 155 million tons a year. In many cases, acid rain is transported by the wind to other regions far from the site where the pollution originates. This phenomenon has made life impossible in tens of thousands of rivers and lakes by changing the chemical composition of the water, and has seriously affected forests and crops, above all in Europe, North America, South America, China and Africa.

There are other wide-ranging problems that affect the deterioration not only of the atmosphere, but of the planet's soil and waters. Many of these problems may not be so new, but they have had high costs in terms of material and human losses, above all in the underdeveloped countries. Poverty has been identified as one of the main threats to environmentally safe development, given that the majority of the world's poor live in ecologically vulnerable areas: 80 percent of the poor in Latin America, 60 percent of the poor in Asia, and 50 percent of the poor in Africa.

There is now a major problem in the quality and distribution of drinking water in underdeveloped nations. As a result of soil erosion, more than 20 million hectares of agricultural land are lost every year worldwide. At the moment, deserts are expanding at the rate of six million hectares per year. Some 3.5 billion hectares of productive land — a surface area roughly equal to that of the

American continent — is presently being affected by desertification, one-third severely. According to the United Nations, this constitutes a threat to the means of subsistence of 850 million people. Recent Food and Agriculture Organization (FAO) figures indicate that deforestation in tropical zones increased from 11.3 million hectares yearly in 1980 to 17 million hectares in 1990.

The loss of biological diversity associated with these processes is a cause of profound concern. The pollution of oceans, seas and coastal zones, as well as the danger to living resources in those areas, constitutes another serious environmental problem.

The problems of cross-border transportation of dangerous wastes deserves special attention, especially when the recipients are underdeveloped countries that don't have the means to adequately treat this residue. Experience seems to demonstrate that the solution cannot be to simply make the transportation of these wastes so expensive that it would become more convenient for the industries in question to reduce their production of such substances.

If the deterioration of the environment is analyzed from an historical perspective, it can be appreciated that the greatest harm to the global ecosystem has been done by the development patterns followed by the most industrialized countries. For their part, the conditions of poverty in which the majority of the world's population lives also have serious effects on the environment and generate an alienating vicious circle between underdevelopment and poverty, on the one hand, and environmental deterioration on the other.

Now that the concept of sustainable development has become widespread, it must be recognized that neither the above-mentioned development patterns of the North nor the underdevelopment of the South are economic systems that are environmentally sustainable. But it would be a mistake to examine each of these two aspects in the same light, even though they are related. This would lead to the absurdity of attributing equal responsibility for environmental deterioration to the citizen of a developed country who earns a relatively high salary, has acquired consumerist habits and has become accustomed to a lifestyle that squanders resources, as to the poor inhabitant of any of the most backward countries of the underdeveloped world, whose daily concern is to find the increasingly scarce means of preventing his or her children from starving to death.

It is difficult for enormous impoverished sectors of the underdeveloped world's population to envisage the satisfaction of future generations' needs when many of their own immediate basic necessities are not even minimally covered. Thus, the pressing environmental preoccupations of the Third World are substantially different from those of the developed countries.

In the most developed countries, where the common preoccupation is the quality of life, there is growing anxiety concerning the medium- or long-term effects of phenomena such as the deterioration of the ozone layer and global warming. In the Third World, however, there has to be a different set of ecological priorities — where in some cases infant mortality reaches levels of 115 deaths for every 1000 live births, where every year 14 million children die before they reach the age of five, where more than a billion people don't have access to the most elementary health services, where life expectancy is less than 63 years, and in the poorest countries less than 52, where more than 300 million children are deprived of their right to schooling, where almost a billion adults are illiterate, where more than 500 million people suffered from hunger in 1990, and where some 180 million children under the age of five suffer from malnutrition. In the Third World, what is in danger is not the quality of life, but life itself and the right to life. These countries' main environmental concerns are the availability of water, the lack of firewood and the exhaustion of agricultural lands.

What practical significance can terms such as ecosystem, biological diversity, impoverishment of the environment and deterioration of the ozone layer have for the illiterate masses deprived of education in the underdeveloped world? How can hundreds of millions of human beings pay attention to these problems when hour after hour, day after day, week after week and year after year of their lives is spent in an anguishing and hopeless struggle to survive?

It is obvious that if we want to truly propose the elimination of the main environmental problems affecting today's world, humanity must take two preliminary steps. For one thing, it must manage to replace the wasteful consumer culture of the industrialized world and of the high-income sectors of underdeveloped countries. This culture can be replaced by a lifestyle that, without sacrificing its present material levels would lead to a more rational use of resources and a significant reduction in the assault on the environment which is present almost everywhere today as a result of that culture. The other step is to conciliate a radical change in the Third World's socioeconomic conditions, and consequently of the living conditions of the impoverished masses of its population. This can come about through a transformation of the present system of international economic relations and the social and economic structures that contribute to the existence of the numerous strata of hungry, sick, dispossessed and ignorant people in the majority of the underdeveloped countries.

This is the only way we can aspire to a thorough solution to the main global ecological problems of the 21st-century, a world that is on our doorstep. But this would require a generalized world consciousness of these causes of environmental problems — in all countries and at all levels within each country. This could generate the political will and indispensable international cooperation needed to effectively confront these problems. Meanwhile, all efforts are worthwhile and should be encouraged and supported, but in the end it will not be the solution our children require and expect from us. They are the ones to whom, if we don't act in time, we will leave the inheritance of an eventually uninhabitable planet.

The vicious circle of underdevelopment and environmental deterioration

As has been demonstrated over and over again, the universal phenomenon of environmental deterioration has its own characteristics and origins, as well as more serious effects, in the countries of the Third World. In those countries, the quest for sustainable development is the quest for development itself, with

development understood not only as growth, but also as the transformation of economic and social structures with the goal of raising the population's quality of life and achieving the gradual formation of new ethical values.

It is precisely this process of development that has been held back in the South, not as a result of accidental events or circumstance, but because of certain type of inherent social relations and ways of organizing production. This situation of backwardness and poverty is, if you will, the most unsustainable aspect of this model of development.

The economic and social crisis that began in the 1980s has greatly accelerated those factors that immediately and foreseeably threaten the human environment — due mainly to a worsening of the international economic order.

The economies of the Third World today still depend on a high level of overexploitation of natural resources. During the last few years, basic commodity exports — including petroleum — were 45 percent of those countries' total exports, with a maximum in Africa of about 90 percent.

Throughout the past decade, these economies have been submitted to a dramatic decapitalization process, through both trade and finance. Consequently, they have seen their chances for sustained economic growth cut off, all this in a context of uncontrollable demographic growth. Therefore, the annual average growth statistic for the gross domestic product of underdeveloped countries has been shrinking over the last three decades, going from 6.1 percent in the period between 1961 and 1973 to barely 2.8 percent in the period between 1983 and 1990. A similar trend can be seen in the per capita figures, which has gone from 3.3 percent in the 1961-1970 period to 0.1 percent in the 1980-1990 period.

Another phenomenon of the crisis which has aggravated environmental deterioration has without a doubt been the increasingly unequal distribution of income between the economies of the North and South — and even within the South itself. Whereas in 1960, 20 percent of the world population with the highest incomes had income levels 30 times higher than those of the poorest 20 percent, by 1990 these levels were 60 times higher. In underdeveloped countries the richest sectors of the population now make up between 10 and 15 percent of the population, while they control most of the economic and natural resources. In Latin America, 10 percent of the population controls 95 percent of arable land.

The major trade problems facing the countries of the Third World, which are generally limited to exporting basic commodities, flow from their constantly diminishing access to the markets of the developed nations. This has come about, among other factors, because of more aggressive protectionist policies, as well as the steady drop in the prices and purchasing power of these products. Between 1980 and 1991, the average price index of 33 basic commodities exported by the underdeveloped nations — excluding fuel — experienced a 50 percent drop. Although future performance is difficult to predict, the World Bank has foreseen that this rate of decrease will be maintained until 1995. In concrete terms, the current prices of these products have been compared by some analysts to those in effect at the turn of the century, and by others to those of the mid-19th century.

Out of a sample of 24 industrialized nations, it was determined that 20 are more protectionist now than they were 10 years ago. This protectionism takes a heavy toll on the underdeveloped nations: $75 billion worth of gross national product are lost annually due to losses in exports.

During the 1980s, the era of the so-called foreign debt crisis, there was a drastic reduction in the flow of financial resources that this group of countries had depended on for decades to finance at least a portion of the most essential investments. In particular, the flow of resources in the form of official aid for development from the countries of the Organization for Economic Cooperation and Development (OECD) is currently less than half of the proposed goal of 0.7 percent of the gross national product of these nations. The underdeveloped nations received barely $44 billion in official aid for development in 1990, while the servicing of the foreign debt — currently calculated at more than $1.3 trillion — has averaged just over $165 billion annually over the last four years.

Thus the servicing of the foreign debt faced by the

underdeveloped nations today is equivalent to three times the amount of official foreign aid they receive. The final result, paradoxically, is that these countries have become net exporters of capital, with figures that have fluctuated between $40 billion and $50 billion annually over the past decade.

In 1990, the UNDP calculated that there were 1.2 billion people living below the poverty line in the Third World. The economic and social situation in the South will continue to deteriorate to the extent that centuries of backwardness and recurrent economic crises offer less and less possibilities of reversing, or at least checking, other consequences of this increase in poverty. These include the uncontrollable demographic growth and unrestrained urbanization characteristic of the Third World.

While the rate of population increase in the industrialized nations averaged 0.8 percent annually between 1960 and 1990, the underdeveloped nations registered a rate of 2.3 percent in the same time period. From 1990 until the year 2000, this rate will continue to be higher in the underdeveloped nations — around two percent, as compared to 0.5 percent in the developed nations — which leads to estimates that 90 percent of the world population growth in the next 10 years will take place in the underdeveloped world.

At the same time, urbanization continues to be more accelerated in the underdeveloped nations, as a result of the constant exodus from rural areas. Between 1960 and 1990, the urban population of the Third World increased at an average annual rate of four percent, compared to a figure of 1.4 percent in the developed nations.

For the 1990-2000 period the rate for the underdeveloped nations will be unchanged, while that of the developed nations will drop to 0.8 percent annually, according to UNDP estimates. This means that by the year 2000, of the 24 cities with populations greater than 10 million inhabitants, 18 will be in underdeveloped nations, and of the six with more than 15 million inhabitants, four will be in this same region.

It must be remembered that in underdeveloped conditions, urbanization takes on a special connotation. The lack of adequate infrastructures results in a disorderly growth of urban concentrations, mainly in the form of slums, with the consequent creation of significant sources of pollution and deterioration of the environment.

Given these conditions, it is all the more urgent that the serious challenge of guaranteeing adequate levels of nutrition to all of the world's inhabitants be taken on and that this be done without causing greater damage to the global environment. It will require tremendous international political will to achieve what has been impossible up until now. At present, 60 percent of the world's inhabitants live in countries with low earnings and insufficient food supplies.

Third World poverty is closely linked to the deterioration of the environment. Dependent on economies based primarily on the exploitation of natural resources, and lacking in both the financial and technological conditions necessary to exploit these resources properly, these nations are quite literally faced with no other alternative for survival than to overexploit these resources. This mismanagement engenders even greater poverty, due to a greater lack of financial and technological resources needed to confront increasingly adverse environmental conditions.

This results in a degrading vicious circle, caught between these two phenomena. In the words of the FAO, it is precisely the resources that are the source of life that are destroyed, not out of ignorance, but simply in order to survive one day more.

The problems of underdevelopment, backwardness, natural disasters and armed conflicts in the underdeveloped world, especially in the 1980s, also contributed to the further deterioration of the environment. This has been exacerbated by the mass migrations of people from some countries to others, or from some regions to others within the same country, and the ensuing overexploitation of natural resources in certain areas. This is further aggravated to the extent that, in general, no measures are taken to protect the environment in these cases.

The most serious ecological consequences of this situation are the impoverishment of the soil, desertification, flooding and drought, exhaustion of clean water supplies, soil loss, deforestation and the loss of biological diversity, as well as the unchecked growth of urban concentrations. The current situation is far worse than that which was observed at the time of the 1972 Conference on the Human Environment.

Today, around 1.3 billion people, or close to 30 percent of the inhabitants of the Third World, do not have access to safe drinking water. More than 2.2 billion lack adequate sanitary services. The situation is worse in rural areas: in 1990, only 63 percent of the rural population of these countries — as compared to 82 percent of the urban population — had access to safe drinking water and only 49 percent of rural inhabitants — compared to 72 percent of their urban counterparts — had access to adequate sanitary facilities.

Furthermore, the underdeveloped world is home to a relentlessly growing number of people whose nutrition depends hypothetically on a fraction of a hectare of arable land, as a result of population growth and soil deterioration. There is no access to financial and technological resources that would allow Third World farmers to increase productivity and crop yields to the extent necessary for maintaining sufficient production in areas already under cultivation. It is obvious that the only short-term solution available to these individuals is to subject new areas to their backward agricultural practices, the direct cause of some of the worst forms of environmental deterioration. An aggravating factor, in some regions of the Third World, is the phenomenon of the displacement of individual farmers from the most productive lands by the extension of large landholdings, or, conversely, the repeated subdivision of land into parcels that are ever more reduced and unviable. Thus another vicious circle closes in around the impoverished farmers of the underdeveloped world, who appear to have no possible escape.

Therefore, to take action in favor of the environment — its conservation and improvement — necessarily means to take action against the causes of the infuriating poverty that continues to ravage the Third World on the eve of the 21st century. This will doubtlessly require a series of socioeconomic transformations — on both national and international levels — which could begin with a just and lasting solution to the problem of the underdeveloped nations' foreign debt and the redirection of available monetary and financial resources toward development.

In this sense, it is obvious that, given the collapse of socialism in Eastern Europe and the disappearance of the Soviet Union, which for many signifies the end of the cold war and the establishment, from a political and military point of view, of a unipolar world, the amount of money spent on armaments, while having begun to decrease, is still excessively high, surpassing $800 billion annually. The underdeveloped nations contribute more than $120 billion to this amount yearly. It is therefore crucial to end this senseless waste of resources on the extermination of humanity and nature, and to redirect them instead to the development and conservation of human and other life.

The environmental interdependence between the underdeveloped world of the South — backward and poor — and the industrialized world of the North is increasingly more obvious, since only one planet exists. The underdeveloped countries have also made the battle for ecological protection of the earth their own. Nonetheless, the strategy of that battle cannot presuppose a separation of environmental problems from problems of economic and social development.

On the contrary, it we want to guarantee a sound ecological future, we must see to it that indiscriminate exploitation of the environment is not accentuated, as it has been until now, by indifference to the right of three-fourths of humanity to develop. Such indifference should be replaced by a recognition of different degrees of responsibility and the establishment of fair and preferential treatment that would give the underdeveloped countries access to the resources and technology necessary to achieve such a goal.

The developed countries' ecological debt

The underdeveloped countries have insisted on the need for an integral focus in the search for solutions to the problems of the environment and development. They have advocated restructuring international economic relations in such a way as to allow those countries access to financial resources and the technologies required to undertake sustainable development programs. From this perspective, the starting point for any negotiations on the environment and development must be the recognition of the ecological debt of the industrialized countries.

Today no person of good faith can deny that the primary factor in the deterioration of the global environment is the model of economic behavior created by the most developed societies and spread by them to the rest of the world — using their own power and the influence of their mechanisms for shaping public opinion. A lifestyle based on the irrational zeal to consume and an absurd pilfering of resources is the main enemy of the environment in these times.

The member states of the OECD represent only 16 percent of the world population and 24 percent of the world's total surface area. Their economies represent 72 percent of the world's gross national product and generate about 76 percent of total world trade, including 73 percent of the exports of chemical products and almost the same proportion of imports of lumber products.

The OECD member countries are, at the same time, responsible for 45 percent of the world carbon dioxide emissions, 40 percent of the world sulphur dioxide emissions and 50 percent of the nitrogen oxide emissions. They produce 60 percent of the industrial wastes in the world and generate 90 percent of the dangerous wastes. In 1984, the United States, the European Community and Japan contributed 86 percent of the world production of chlorofluorocarbons, while the Third World countries produced only 4.4 percent.

The OECD countries utilize 52 percent of the total energy produced commercially, including 50 percent of the fossil fuels and 56 percent of the oil consumed in the world. Of the 10 countries which generate most of the gas emissions that cause the greenhouse effect, five are highly industrialized. If the former Soviet Union is included, this group would be responsible for over 40 percent of the total emissions. The United States, which has the greatest emissions, produces 17.6 percent of the world total. The developed countries' contribution to the greenhouse effect is four times higher than that of the Third World.

Historically, the developed countries have been the main promoters and beneficiaries of deforestation in the underdeveloped countries. Under the colonial regimes and following the economic expansion of the great capitalist powers

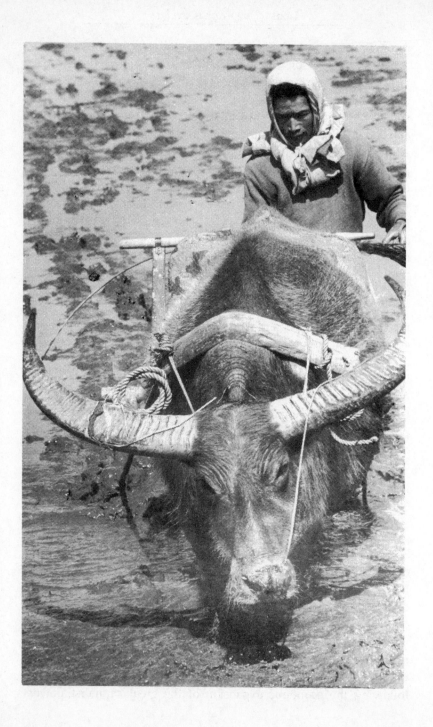

and the neocolonial exploitation of the Third World's natural resources, there was indiscriminate felling of vast forest areas in the world. This was carried out in order to utilize the lumber and also to convert this forest land into agricultural land for the production of food and raw materials which could be exported to those industrialized countries.

Analyzing this from a broader perspective, the inevitable conclusion is that the ultimate responsibility for the cumulative environmental deterioration in the Third World as a whole belongs to the developed capitalist world — and especially those countries which by means of colonial and neocolonial exploitation were to blame throughout history for the backwardness and deformation of the economies of countries in Africa, Asia and Latin America. As has already been pointed out, these have been and continue to be the ultimate causes of the most generalized and most acute environmental problems in the Third World.

The principal producers of pesticides, fertilizers and other noxious chemical products, even after they have been banned, continue to be the developed countries.

Although the industrialized countries have not been the only ones directly or indirectly associated with war and its preparation, they have a large responsibility for generating the enormous volume of resources in the world wasted on these activities, and the consequent environmental deterioration and modifications of ecosystems in many regions of the planet. During the Vietnam war alone, over 80,000 metric tons of the defoliant called Agent Orange were released in that country, with disastrous consequences for the physical environment and human health. Radioactive contamination, resulting from nuclear explosions and accidents, is associated principally with the industrialized countries. It has been estimated that 20 percent of the industrial pollution of the most developed countries comes from factories linked to military production. Prospecting and extracting the enormous volumes of most of the minerals needed for military activity has an environmental impact much greater than that of other mining activities.

All too frequently, in developed capitalist societies it is clear that ecological concerns are incompatible with the profit principle, the exaggerated desire to consume and the primary objective of individual well-being, which are the essential driving forces of those societies. In transportation, for example, technical achievements in conserving the environment have been negated by the uncontrolled growth of those means of transportation, especially automobiles. Seventy-eight percent of all highway vehicles in the world are found in the industrialized countries.

One of the deficiencies of environmental control policies in many developed countries is the retroactive application and scope of some regulations. In these countries there are still some 100,000 chemical compounds with potentially dangerous effects which are used commercially and which, because they existed before certain legislation was passed, are not banned. Furthermore, other chemical compounds have been banned within those countries, but their export is permitted to other regions of the world.

Environmental protection measures have been incorporated into the economic foreign policies of some industrialized countries in such a way that they have had a serious impact on underdeveloped economies. For instance, since the mid-1980s there has been a growing tendency to condition economic aid to developing countries with the need for both countries to allegedly share responsibility for the environment. Strictly speaking, such aid should be granted on the basis of a recognition of the historical responsibility of developed countries for the Third World's economic underdevelopment and environmental deterioration, and not seen as something linked to goals that can never be achieved.

Historically, the developed countries have contributed to the export of pollution to the Third World. Since the 1960s, this method has been utilized to transfer the ecological cost of certain technologies. This has taken place directly, through the export of industrial wastes and other noxious compounds, and indirectly, through the transfer of polluting technologies and imposing wasteful models for consumption and economic structure on underdeveloped countries.

Sending toxic wastes to the Third World constitutes one direct method of exporting pollution from the North to the South. Often the precarious situation of underdeveloped economies is used as a pretext to offer financing or other resources in short supply in exchange for accepting toxic wastes. In most cases there is no guarantee of their proper handling in the receiving countries. In other cases, acid rain, produced basically by the emissions of industrial pollutants in the developed countries, is carried by winds to areas very distant from its source, affecting quite a few underdeveloped countries.

The transnational corporations have been responsible, to a large degree, for the process of transferring polluting technologies to underdeveloped countries, principally since the 1960s. Because of the need to receive investment resources and technology and because of the very models of development adopted by the South or imposed on it in the last three decades, environmental regulations are often lax in those countries, thus favoring the importation of such polluting technologies. In the underdeveloped countries, transnational corporations are active in very environmentally sensitive sectors, such as mining, oil drilling, agribusiness, the manufacture of chemical products, refining heavy metals and automobile manufacturing, among others.

In essence, the North's ecological deterioration has been exported — in large measure to the South, as part of a long process of capitalist development. And it is precisely in the weak underdeveloped economies where the harmful effects of the impoverishment of the environment combine with high levels of poverty and economic dependence, promoting the socioeconomic vulnerability of those nations. It is now up to the developed and rich world to pay its ecological debt to the underdeveloped and poor masses of humanity, through cooperation, financial and technical assistance and the transfer of environmentally clean technologies. To do so would be an act of historical justice and ultimately a demonstration of goodwill and a contribution to its own future well-being and development.

Global warming, underdevelopment and the energy crisis

According to some estimates, 49 percent of the gases causing the greenhouse effect come from the energy sector, 24 percent from industry, 14 percent from deforestation and 13 percent from agriculture. Today, humankind consumes some 161 million barrels of petroleum every day — 150 years ago the world consumption was eight million. It is estimated that by the year 2010 the demand for energy will increase by between 50 and 60 percent.

As we all know, the predominance of fossil fuels — coal, petroleum and natural gas — in energy consumption makes this sector responsible for half of the greenhouse effect. Altogether, fossil fuels represent more than 90 percent of the world balance of commercial energy. Carbon dioxide is considered as the gas principally responsible for the greenhouse effect — in more than 70 percent of cases it come from the use of fossil-fuels. The energy sector alone emits 21 billion tons of this gas every year.

As a result, the measures for controlling climatic change are directed, in the main, toward modifying current patterns of energy production and consumption.

At an international level, the main countries responsible for global warming are the industrialized nations, which have based their development, to a great extent, on intensive consumption of fossil fuels. Conservative estimates show that the highly industrialized nations, with only 15 percent of the world's population, absorb 50 percent of world fossil fuel consumption and give out more than half of world emissions of gases which cause the greenhouse effect.

As far as the underdeveloped countries are concerned, where three-quarters of the world's population live, they absorb less than 18 percent of world fossil fuel consumption. The per capita ratio between consumption of fossil fuels in highly industrialized and underdeveloped countries is eight to one. According to specialized sources, the main contribution to global warming made by underdeveloped nations is through carbon dioxide emissions associated with deforestation. This process is provoked, in part, by the inefficient and irrational use of traditional biomass fuels, such as firewood, in many Third World countries. Today, around 70 percent of the population of underdeveloped countries uses firewood for fuel. It is estimated that by the year 2000, around 2.4 billion people will be living in areas where there is a great shortage of firewood.

When it comes to deciding who is responsible for global warming, it is impossible to compare the effects of tropical deforestation and the emissions of methane derived from certain crops in underdeveloped countries, with the emission of polluting gases from other sources in developed countries. What is really needed is a treatment which differentiates between these, since they are two very distinct phenomena. While the majority of emissions from the Third World are conditioned by the state of underdevelopment and poverty these countries find themselves in, the emissions from the industrialised North have been, to a great extent, the result of an excessive and wasteful energy consumption.

Energy conservation programs in the Third World have been extremely limited due, among other things, to the severe financial and technological restrictions facing these countries. In 1989, petroleum consumption per unit of gross domestic product in this group of countries was almost 65 percent greater than that of the developed nations. The energy crisis these countries face is one of low per capita levels of commercial energy consumption, lack of modern and diversified networks and enormous debt in this sector of the economy. There is also the problem of high energy inefficiency, the limited development of fresh and renewable resources and the difficulty of assimilating new technologies, such as nuclear energy. Faced with this reality, the majority of the Third World population has no alternative but to damage the environment, just in order to survive. For example, an African family uses five times more energy in preparing food than does a European household.

Some writers have shown that underdeveloped countries could reach a standard of living similar to that enjoyed by Western European Countries in the 1970s without any need for a substantial increase in per capita energy consumption. This scenario supposes the use of more efficient energy technologies and, therefore, the investment of great sums of money to replace the current structure of energy consumption based, in the majority of cases, on the irrational use of traditional biomass fuels, such as firewood and vegetable and animal waste.

Due to all this, the energy sector should be a priority area when it comes to evaluating the financial and technological requirements of the Third World, in order to break the vicious circle that exists between the energy crisis, technological underdevelopment and environmental deterioration. Within the framework of international negotiations on climatic change, the underdeveloped countries have generally advocated the creation of a worldwide system for the transfer of financial and environmentally suitable technological resources which would allow these nations to reduce emissions of greenhouse gases and, at the same time, establish the bases for a sustained economic development. In this context, the levels of greenhouse gas emissions, so unequally balanced between developed and underdeveloped countries, should be the starting point of negotiations. They should be analyzed from an historical point of view, which recognizes the cumulative effect of environmental damage caused by the industrialized countries' emissions. In the same way, the principle must be observed that everyone on the planet has the same right to atmospheric resources, and therefore transmission levels set must be based on a per capita distribution.

Among the many initiatives begun to limit greenhouse gas emissions, the two proposals which have generated the most debate are the setting of taxes on the consumption of different energy sources (based on the carbon content of each) and permits to emit gases, which could be commercialized at an international level in accordance with the laws of the market.

Some studies argue that by applying taxes on carbon emissions, the internal energy prices in developed countries would increase, resulting in a slowing down of the growth rate of these economies. What would follow would be a reduction in the main external markets of the underdeveloped countries, creating additional financial pressures on these nations with increased inflation, a rise in international interest rates and a reduction in the world credit flow. Some estimates show that for every annual percentage drop in economic activity on the part of the OECD countries, the economic growth of the underdeveloped countries is reduced by 0.7 percent. This demonstrates the high level of subordination and dependence of the underdeveloped economies on the industrialized North.

According to a study carried out by the secretariat of OPEC, the gross domestic product of the underdeveloped countries would show cumulative losses of between $600 million and $3.7 billion in the 1991-2010 period, as a result of a carbon tax applied by the OECD. A considerable part of these losses would be felt by energy exporting countries, which would see notable reductions in their foreign exchange earnings. In the underdeveloped countries not part of OPEC, the average annual growth rate of the gross domestic product in the 1991-2010 period would decline by between 0.1 and 0.8 percent. These countries, the vast majority of which are net importers of energy, would nevertheless feel a certain amount of relief with the reduction of world petroleum prices which could come about as a result of putting into practice the OECD carbon taxes.

With the widespread application of these policies in the OECD, the developed countries should take on their responsibility in compensating for the losses that the underdeveloped countries could suffer as a result of this measure. Some studies sponsored by the United Nations suggest that part of the funds raised by this taxation policy should be diverted to the Third World, to finance sustainable development. Otherwise, the underdeveloped nations would be the ones to take on a substantial part of the cost of adjustment which undoubtedly the developed world should put into practice in order to alleviate environmental damage.

There is also the danger of producing a relocation or displacement of those activities which intensively emit carbon within the countries of the OECD to other areas of the world, where the taxes would be lower or nonexistent. This would reinforce the tendency to transfer polluting technologies to the Third World, and, consequently, would cancel, at least partially, the effect of the tax policies on global emissions of carbon dioxide. For this reason, the taxation policies should be accompanied by regulations covering the activities of transnational companies beyond their countries of origin, so that such companies make a commitment to sustainable development.

As far as the emission permits are concerned, they constitute a market mechanism which, in the judgment of its promoters, represents the most effective way to control carbon dioxide emissions and, at the same time, to secure the financial resources required by underdeveloped countries in order to face the problems of underdevelopment and environmental damage. Those who support this mechanism point out that with the granting of emission permits for each country based on per capita quotas, most of the underdeveloped countries would be given permits for more than their short-term levels of emission and they could, therefore, sell them to those industrialized countries which have exceeded their quotas. In that way, the underdeveloped countries would receive substantial financial resources, which could be invested in technological programs and policies aimed at adjusting to a lower level of emissions. In turn, the developed countries would be encouraged to increase their energy efficiency and transfer more efficient energy technologies to the nations of the Third World.

Nevertheless, behind the apparent good intentions of this proposal, there lies an enormous danger for the underdeveloped nations. Faced with their severe financial restrictions and, given the greater decision-making power of the developed countries, a large number of the emission permits for the underdeveloped countries could be sold off at bargain prices. A significant part of the income made on such sales could be taken up by paying off the foreign debt or other financial deficits, without having any significant impact on the development of environmentally safe technologies. It would probably not be long before people would be encouraging the exchange of debt for emission permits, which would undoubtedly have serious implications for the Third World.

It is not a coincidence, although it is worrisome, that in the midst of the wave of neoliberalism currently sweeping the planet, attempts should be made to give market mechanisms a central role in solving environmental problems. Under the conditions of this plan to commercialize emission permits — or rather, pollution permits — the socioeconomic activity of the underdeveloped countries could be seriously limited, to the extent that they sell the permits without carrying out the structural adjustments required to improve energy efficiency in particular and the economy in general. In the framework of the emerging new world order, this would be one of the possible manipulations of the sustainable development theory in favor of the interests of the developed countries and the reinforcement of the subordinate and dependent relationship of the underdeveloped South to the industrialized North.

Biological diversity and development

Humans have constantly affected the natural habitat of living species — including their own — in their adaptation to the world, through their search for food, energy and clothing, among other things. However, as a result of the depredatory behavior of humans, the process of habitat alteration and the consequent disappearance of plant, animal and microorganism species is taking place at a much greater speed today. It has been calculated that the rate of species loss in 1980 was one a day and in 1990, one an hour.

In general terms, it is estimated that perhaps around 250,000 species — a quarter of the earth's total biological diversity — are in serious danger of becoming extinct within the next 20 or 30 years. Some specialists suggest that around 350 species of birds, 200 species of mammals and around 25,000 plant species are on the verge of extinction. The loss of these world genetic resources is the most serious and irreparable consequence of deforestation and of global environmental deterioration.

This problem, perhaps more than any that make up the so-called ecological crisis, is linked to the phenomenon of underdevelopment. The underdeveloped countries, because of the geographical area they occupy, possess the world's main natural resources and the greatest and most varied biological reserves. At the same time, they are caught up in socioeconomic conditions which are favorable to overexploitation. In the tropical rainforests, for example, which are home for up to 90 percent of the world's biological diversity, the process of species extinction and altered habitat has accelerated largely as a result of advancing deforestation.

Other habitats rich in species also in danger of extinction are the coral reefs, as well as lakes with long geological histories and salt marshes. The coral reefs in particular, which spread some 400,000 square kilometers worldwide and play host to an estimated half million species, are suffering the effects of global warming, pollution of the oceans and human depredation. The rate of damage threatens to leave very few remains by the beginning of the next century. This would mean an enormous loss of important organisms and toxins for medical science.

The loss of biological diversity is also identified with the deterioration of genetic diversity within each species, a phenomenon which implies the progressive reduction and possible disappearance of the variability of species and races. It is paradoxical to note that, just when science and technology are allowing us to explore and exploit to a much greater extent the genetic variability of all vegetable and animal species, this natural variability should find itself so threatened. And what is worse is the alarming rate at which species, of which we know very little or nothing, are diminishing or disappearing. Until now, scientists have only carried out intensive research on one in a hundred plant species and on an even smaller proportion of animal species. At the current rate, countless species will disappear before humans can even know them or benefit from their unknown potentials. This would have serious ecological and economic consequences.

Socioeconomic and above all technological factors have influenced this process. It is recognized today that, as a result of the so-called Green Revolution, agriculture became highly dependent upon chemical products, with serious implications for the environment. In addition, this created the conditions for the deterioration of genetic diversity, as a result of cultivating high-yield hybrids.

It has also been increasingly emphasized that the accelerated development of biotechnology over the last few years could have positive and negative implications for the loss of biological diversity in the foreseeable future, especially in its applications in the food industry. It is possible to predict, with further advances made in techniques for genetic manipulation — and in fact, such progress has already been made — this improvement of plants and animals. To name but a few applications, are their possibilities for adaptation to the environment as well as their productive possibilities, the incorporation into production of lands which are currently sterile, and even the production of food from non-natural raw materials. This all goes to show the need to conserve this variability, as the only way of guaranteeing the biological source for genetic engineering.

Today more than ever, the underdeveloped countries urgently need access to knowledge, to scientific and technological development. This is not only because it would allow them to solve infinite economic, social and ecological problems, but because, in the current stage of capitalist development, scientific knowledge plays a principal role in the accumulation of capital. Modern biotechnology could be a path toward economic development and the satisfaction of many of the food, energy and health needs of the countries of the South, whose ecosystems have the greatest biological diversity and who have the greatest number of so-called centers of phytogenic diversity.

Through the possibilities presented by the development of modern biotechnology, the genetic resources of the underdeveloped world have gained extraordinary value. This has come about in a context of great technological dependence of these countries and their very precarious systems of protection against the commercial appropriation of their genetic material.

The essential features of modern biotechnological development do not seem to point toward a net benefit for the underdeveloped countries, which would be the producers most in need of this new technology. Just as with the Green Revolution, the poor producers of the Third World would not have general access to these developments; neither would their dependence on imported goods be reduced. Furthermore, with the process of saving and substituting raw materials now made increasingly possible in the industrialized countries by advances in biotechnology — and technology in general — the main exports of the Third World are being severely hit.

In fact, the possession and control of genetic resources constitutes a new way of plundering the Third World, which has become the main objective of those transnational corporations involved in this field. The monopoly which these large corporations have over advanced biotechnological research means that, in practice, they do not work on what is most urgently needed but on what offers the greatest commercial possibilities. The seed sector is a good example. The expansion of the major chemical and pharmaceutical transnationals into the seed industry leaves Third World producers in a position of greater subordination and dependence, as buyers of a more expensive technological package designed with the interests of these firms in mind rather than the economic and ecological interests of agricultural production in underdeveloped countries.

The private nature of advanced biotechnological research in the developed world means this work is being carried out with greater and greater secrecy, since their main objective is to create a new patentable product and in that way appropriate technological income. This constitutes a great obstacle to the transfer of technology to underdeveloped countries, as well as hindering access to higher academic centers for their scientists.

The privatization boom, together with the need to maximize profit, are having a growing impact on the new mechanisms for controlling copyrights of biotechnological advances, and even on the control of the national heritage of the underdeveloped countries. Attempts are being made to impose a patent system on the underdeveloped countries which, firstly, does not recognize the right of these countries to enjoy the profits made. These countries are the living source for new knowledge and for hundreds of years have contributed to quite a considerable extent to its improvement and natural selection. Secondly, it will be even more difficult, above all financially, for the underdeveloped nations to have access to such advances. The most serious question is that, with the extension of market forces to the problems of conservation of biological diversity, we could be setting out on a path toward the loss of national sovereignty over natural resources.

Out of the concern for the loss or erosion of biological diversity come the proposals for its conservation. All the specialists agree on the prime importance of conserving the ecosystems and species in their natural environment, but the underdeveloped countries generally lack the financial resources needed for this. The offsite conservation of germ plasm is currently carried out in more than 450 institutions worldwide. Fifty percent of the samples collected are in industrialized countries, 21 percent in germ plasm banks belonging to international centers and 29 percent in underdeveloped countries.

There is now strong pressure in favor of privatizing the collections of international agricultural research centers which, like those linked to the FAO and UNESCO, have until now allowed free access to their genetic resources. The World Bank has recommended that these centers establish cooperation agreements with the private sector for obtaining financial resources and the application of patents and other forms of copyright. Many of the FAO's own initiatives to protect free access to phytogenic resources have come up against the interests of transnational companies and the industrialized countries.

It is for all these reasons that the negotiations for a biological diversity convention, as part of the preparatory process of this Rio Summit, have caused particular concern among underdeveloped countries. It all appears to indicate that the developed countries, especially the United States, plan to arrive at an agreement which would guarantee them free access to and greater control over what are the national and sovereign resources of the underdeveloped countries, without recognizing their rights as owners of biological and genetic resources which are important sources of knowledge and scientific and technological development. At the same time, the highly industrialized countries are trying to gain in the Uruguay Round an even tighter control over copyrights and biotechnological advances.

It is not too much to insist that any biological diversity treaty favoring in a preferential manner the interests of the industrialized countries — as well as any separate attempt on the part of these states to impose declarations of principle in this matter — would not only threaten the sovereignty of the underdeveloped countries, but would also constitute legal instruments which could serve to reinforce the conditional nature of economic aid to the Third World. Indeed, if any alteration of living organisms can be patented and thus generate profit, how would the underdeveloped countries be compensated for their

contribution of genetic diversity that is the basis for obtaining genetic modifications? How can the Third World protect its natural resources and, in particular, its biological diversity, to help in its own development?

Financial resources and the transfer of technology

According to preliminary estimates, the underdeveloped countries as a whole would need no fewer than an additional $40 billion per year to invest in programs aimed at achieving environmental sustainability, on the basis of economic activity levels for 1990. This sum represents 25 percent of the total foreign debt payments made by these countries that year. In the year 2000, the figure needed will be almost $60 billion.

Certain ecological organizations have proposed that it would take some $125 billion a year in aid to the Third World between now and the end of the century to put Agenda 21 into practice, not counting the efforts that would have to be carried out by the underdeveloped countries themselves. Another estimate concludes that if the Third World's needs for environmental protection are added to those for socially indispensable growth, the amount of supplementary capital needed would rise from some $60 billion in 1990 to close to $140 billion in the year 2000.

Taking into account the magnitude of the resources needed and the serious financial restrictions suffered by underdeveloped countries, the possibility of investing large sums in the environment depends above all on a just and lasting solution of the serious problems faced by these economies. These include the enormous foreign debt burden, the transfer of resources abroad that is part of the debt problem, the trade barriers that prevent the access of these countries' goods to world markets on an equal footing, and the existing limitations on technology transfers to the Third World. No one denies these countries' need to design their own strategies for socioeconomic development that would allow them to ensure sustained expansion of their productive capacity, confront their serious social problems, correct their environmental problems and avoid an eventual deterioration of the environment, in accordance with their available resources. Nevertheless, it is evident that external financing must play a significant role. This is the primary way of paying the developed world's ecological debt.

External financing for sustainable development cannot be the result of a redistribution of the already meager financial resources that are sent to the Third World, but must be a flow of new capital. Otherwise, the environmental issue would merely become another condition for development aid. Furthermore, this flow of additional capital must be granted under favorable repayment conditions, both with respect to interest rates and payment schedules, including the possible granting of credits that do not have to be paid back.

According to certain calculations, in order to cover the pledged amounts of official development aid and the additional financial resources needed by the underdeveloped countries for environmental purposes, developed countries should earmark no less than one percent of their gross national product per year as "official aid for sustainable development." This would imply an additional contribution by developed countries of at least 0.3 percent of their gross national product to the Third World's environmental programs. These figures do not include the financial flow toward the former socialist countries of Eastern Europe. Nevertheless, the truth is that, with very few exceptions, developed countries have been hesitant to make concrete commitments to additional financing for sustainable development.

In discussions on the need for additional resources that would be invested in the environment, a concept often brought into play is that of "association for additional aid." This refers to the need to achieve a better articulation of the developing countries' policies and strategies among themselves as a precondition for stimulating the flow of financial resources toward environmental programs. Without a doubt, any attempt to achieve a better coordination of economic policies among underdeveloped nations tends to make them more complementary, above all in the context of economic integration schemes. But if the idea of "association for additional aid" were used as a pretense for generalizing neoliberal formulas throughout the Third World with the goal of attracting foreign capital, then the counterproductive effects of such an attempt would exert a severely negative influence on the socioeconomic future of these countries.

One of the new financing mechanisms that is often mentioned in recent times is the so-called exchange of debt for environmental protection. According to this principle, part of the foreign debt of an underdeveloped country can be bought on the market by foreign governments or nongovernmental agencies with a given discount margin. The value of this sold debt in national currency, sometimes with discounts, can then be invested in the debtor country's environmental protection programs, which would include, among other things, the establishment of protected areas.

Up until now, the tangible effect of these programs has been quite limited. According to a U.S. Congressional report, a total of 26 operations of this kind were carried out in 13 underdeveloped countries between 1986 and 1990. The nominal amount of the debt saved was $126 million, which amounts to less than 0.05 percent of those countries' total debt. Two-thirds of the exchanged debt was in one country, Costa Rica, whose total debt was only reduced by some two percent in this fashion.

Exchanging the debt for environmental protection, independently of the good intentions of the environmentalists, does not resolve either of the two problems that it links together. In the first place, it does not solve the problem of the debt insofar as it fails to tackle the causes that generate it. However, above all, it entails a potential loss of sovereignty on the part of the country in question, especially when the agreements reached limit the rights of the debtor state over certain natural resources or areas that are declared to be protected by way of this procedure. This mechanism also suffers from the negative aspects common to all forms of capitalization of the foreign debt, including, among others, the inflationary impact on the debtor nation's economy. In general, these programs place priority on projects that serve the interests of the party promoting them or that have international repercussions. In many cases, these are not the projects that are of greatest interest to the underdeveloped nations, as they do not provide obvious, immediate benefits to the population of the country in question.

Another option that has been studied, in addition to bilateral agreements on the exchange of debt for environmental protection, is the creation of a multilateral entity that would use a centralized fund to purchase debts at a lowered rate and then use the titles acquired to finance sustainable development projects through negotiations with the debtor nations. Yet even under this model it is evident that programs for exchanging debt for environmental protection are far from being the ideal mechanism to link together a just solution to the debt problem with efforts to confront the environmental problems of the Third World.

The serious financial difficulties faced by the underdeveloped nations in confronting the problems of the environment and development take on special significance because of the existing limitations of the transfer of environmentally sound technology to the Third World. During the past decade — characterized by the negative impact of the foreign debt on the Third World — there has been a flow of international finance away from these countries and, consequently, a flow of technology transfers. This has had an effect on the trading of capital goods, as well as on direct foreign investment and technical assistance.

Due to the fragility of the ecosystems of the underdeveloped nations and the lack of resources available for them to confront the deterioration of the environment, the transfer of environmentally sound technology is an essential component of sustainable development. The most frequent obstacles to the transfer of advanced technology to the underdeveloped nations — aside from financial restrictions that flow directly or indirectly from the problem of debt — include the lack of information, a skilled labor force, and the necessary infrastructure to assure the spread of new technologies.

As a consequence of the profound transformations brought about by the current scientific and technological revolution, there have been significant changes in the corporate strategies of transnational companies. These corporate strategies promote the formation of strategic alliances among firms in the developed nations in order to confront the rising costs of research and development and to guarantee greater protection of copyrights. This lessens the transfer of technology to the Third World.

These new corporate strategies have met with strong support from the industrialized nations. In effect, the governments of these countries, particularly that of the United States, have pushed strongly in the Uruguay Round for stricter and more uniform norms regarding the protection of intellectual property rights.

The establishment of these kinds of protective measures would result in rising costs for imported technology, especially in the industries that make intensive use of patented procedures. This entails additional demands for financial resources in the underdeveloped nations, which must be taken into account where, new agreements and protocols are signed for the protection of the environment.

At the same time, the fact that the demand for environmentally sound technology is largely determined by the specific geographic and socioeconomic conditions of the underdeveloped nations means that, in many cases, this technology cannot be transferred from abroad. As a result, there is a need for the development of an endogenous technological capacity, which would permit, in addition to the assimilation, adaptation and development of imported technologies, the creation of new domestic expertise and technologies.

Given the financial and technological vulnerability of the underdeveloped nations, it is crucial that international agreements be reached to guarantee the basic conditions necessary for the shift of the economies of the South toward patterns for sustainable development. The alternative is the perpetuation of the vicious circle of underdevelopment, poverty and environmental destruction, with serious ecological, economic and social consequences not only for the Third World, but for all of humanity.

Sustainable development and the environment

Taking advantage of the radical changes in the balance of world economic and political forces, the industrialized nations insist on the global character of environmental problems with the obvious intention of watering down their own considerable responsibilities. They then use this situation to demand onerous concessions from the Third World. In this way, the process of internationalizing the ecological movement is converted into one more element of the new world order.

As is well-known, in the heat of international debate and in the context of internationalizing ecological consciousness, much has been made of the concept of "sustainable development" — understood as development capable of satisfying the needs of the present without compromising the ability of future generations to meet their own needs. The concept aspires to a superior form of development, one that is more equitable and humane.

The wisdom of the concept of sustainable development lies in placing the ecology within a relevant context, and its focus on the need for global action that looks beyond the present to recognize the urgency to protect the natural basis for life for future generations. Poverty is recognized to be an inequality that must by dealt with as a whole. Demographic growth is correctly viewed as a consequence of squalor. Ecology and development are seen as interconnected parts, not irreconcilable.

Nevertheless, despite its widely growing acceptance, the thesis of sustainable development is not free from contradictions and limitations. One of these is its ambiguous character, in that it identifies the existing social disparities in the world today, but does not recognize the mechanisms that have generated this inequality. A consistent interpretation of sustainable development should begin with the recognition that underdevelopment is the result of the plundering of the Third World. This plundering has been prolonged in our time by an international economic order that uses the mechanisms of debt, unfair division of the world's labor, trade protectionism and control over the flow of finances to heighten the exploitation of the underdeveloped nations and, as a consequence, the ensuing ecological destruction.

Moreover, there is a tendency to view sustainable development as a formula for the reconciliation of environmental conservation, social equality, economic growth and market forces. It is clear that many are attempting to envelop the concept of sustainable development in the aura of a new utopia. What is equally clear is the potential danger for the socioeconomic future of the underdeveloped countries posed by the related concept of the so-called "green market." According to this concept, market forces alone will guarantee stable and equitable socioeconomic and environmental development. The concept of the green market —

which reflects the disastrous influence of neoliberalism on discussions of the environment and development — tends to favor those economic agents seeking to legitimize the right to cause damage to the environment and to commercialize this right.

Another significant limitation that has been imposed on the thesis of sustainable development is the suggestion that the same multilateral agencies dominated by the most developed nations, largely responsible for the activities that have caused the greatest damage to the environment, should now guide the transition to a harmonious, equitable and environmentally sound development. However, sustainable development depends on an international climate of understanding, justice and equality. There is no doubt that the recognition of the major environmental challenges facing the world tends to unite nations in the search for common solutions. However, this consensus disappears when the time comes to specify the responsibilities among nations and to establish commitments to international cooperation, such as trade regulations, external financial aid and the transfer of technology.

The international rise of neoliberal theory and practice, beginning in the early 1980s, and the resurgence of old theories of the "perfect market" have had a considerable effect on world debate on the environment. The resurgence of the philosophy of the free play of market forces as the infallible formula for correcting economic imbalances has been promoted by certain conservative political forces that have held sway since the beginning of the last decade in some of the most powerful of the highly industrialized nations, such as the United States and Great Britain.

International practice has demonstrated that the active participation of government in the preservation of natural resources is crucial. However, those who promote the idea of the green market minimize the role of the state in the protection of the environment and ignore the contradiction between short-term commercial interests, which tend to accelerate the depredation of natural resources, and the need to conserve those resources, in the long-term interests of society.

There are certain countries and forces currently seeking to impose the green market on the relations between developed and underdeveloped countries, with the pretext of confronting global environmental challenges. This is true, for example, of the proposal to establish and commercialize international permits for the emission of polluting gases, a situation which, if it became widespread, would have serious negative effects on the future of the underdeveloped countries.

The growing influence of neoliberal policies are cause for considerable concern, especially when these policies are imposed on underdeveloped nations, or when they are incorporated into North-South relations. An obvious example is the highly negative environmental impact that has resulted from the monetarist, restrictive and privatizing focus of the macroeconomic programs recommended by the International Monetary Fund for debtor nations. As a means of securing payments for the servicing of the foreign debt, these programs have promoted, among other measures, cuts in public spending and the use of any means possible to achieve a balance in foreign trade. Similarly, based on the neoliberal premise that state activity is intrinsically inefficient, state participation in the economy is reduced to a minimum, and wide-scale privatization is promoted.

When cuts are made in public spending, investment in environmental conservation is among the first to be held back. Furthermore, as a result of the efforts to achieve a trade balance at any cost, the volume of exports is frequently increased without regard for the overexploitation of both renewable and nonrenewable natural resources. Furthermore, these desperate efforts are not always successful.

A number of recent studies based on an analysis of the socioeconomic impact of IMF adjustment programs have revealed that the organization's formulas not only ignore the problems of poverty and the environment, but also encourage a total disregard for both in the underdeveloped nations. One of these studies shows that of 48 adjustment programs put into practice by the IMF between 1986 and 1990, 78 percent included reductions in public spending, especially in the social sector. These demands were complied with by the governments of the debtor nations in the following ways: in 92 percent of cases, cuts were made in spending on housing, public health or economic assistance to the population; in 62 percent of the cases, spending was reduced in two out of three of these sectors; and in 29 percent of cases, cuts of over 20 percent were made on all social spending.

As a consequence, these programs not only have a direct environmental cost, but are also a fundamental factor in the increase in social inequality, and especially in poverty, in the underdeveloped nations over recent years. In this way, they further contribute indirectly to the deterioration of the environment. Neoliberal formulas are, without a doubt, a fundamental link added in the 1980s to the chain of factors responsible for the structural poverty that has plagued the economies of underdeveloped nations since their inception.

Cuba's ecological policy and reality

Concern for protection and conservation of natural resources, considered the property of all the people, began in Cuba with the revolutionary victory of 1959. In those first years, special efforts were made to expand the forests, which were devastated in the colonial period and during the expansion of the large sugarcane plantations and cattle ranches.

In Cuba, a socialist country, the environment and natural resources are considered the common heritage of all society and are therefore the interest of the nation as a whole. Concern for environmental problems is manifested throughout society. The Constitution of the Republic, put into effect in 1976 following approval in a popular referendum, expressly stipulates that it is the responsibility of the state and of each citizen to protect the country's environment and natural resources. In 1981, the National Assembly of People's Power, the highest legislative organ in the country, approved the Environmental Protection and Rational Use of Natural Resources Act. Continuing the country's efforts to create a system of environmental protection standards, in 1990 the National Protection System was created.

In 1977, the National Commission for Environmental Protection and the Rational Use of Natural Resources was established, made up of representatives of different state agencies and sectors of civil society. In 1980, similar commissions were organized in all the country's provinces and municipalities.

The radical changes generated by the Cuban Revolution have had direct benefits for the environment, by transforming living conditions and in this way creating the prerequisites so that people are not forced to act against the environment. Access to work, the development of a broad-based health care system centering on human well-being and the considerable rise in the population's general educational level and technical and professional training have been fundamental factors in environmental protection.

On these solid social bases, throughout these 30 years of revolution, Cuba has had major environmental achievements, such as the creation and proper utilization of hydraulic resources, the creation of a vast network of parks and protected areas, the application of coherent policies for the protection of flora and fauna and the preservation of biological diversity, among the many achievements that could be mentioned. However, there are still environmental problems in Cuba and work is underway to control and eliminate them.

An important example is the pollution of bays. In the case of Havana Bay, Cuba has had invaluable international cooperation in the diagnosis of the problem and is beginning to solve it. Work has also been carried out to reverse some soil erosion and degradation, in particular in mining areas, as well as some local problems involving the pollution of surface waters from the waste of the sugar industry.

Advances have been made in the recovery of beaches and coastal areas damaged by erosion. One project of considerable magnitude is the Southern Dike in Havana province, recently completed. This will stop and reverse the salinization of tens of thousands of hectares of land which could be used for agriculture. It will also recover hydraulic resources which are extremely important in meeting the needs for water in agriculture and industry and for the population of the provinces of Havana and the City of Havana.

Given the strategic priority assigned to tourism, all the infrastructure projects carried out in beaches, cays and other potential tourist areas are undertaken following a careful evaluation of the possible environmental impact, and the ecological implications of each investment are constantly and closely watched. Of course, Cuba's favorable environmental conditions are a fundamental premise for the development of the tourism industry, including a considerable component of ecological tourism.

Another environmental field which receives priority attention in Cuba is that of seabeds. The strict measures to protect coral reefs are especially notable.

The creation and ongoing encouragement of environmental awareness is one of the most important weapons for protecting the environment in today's Cuba. The consistent application of these policies has had some significant successes: the surface areas covered by forests has increased in the last 30 years from 14 to 20 percent of the country's land and 1.5 billion trees will planted in this five-year period. In Cuba there are no significant problems of atmospheric contamination.

In the 1960s the first actions were taken in the country's mountainous . areas to establish an integrated use of natural resources. Today this program, combined with environmental protection, is aimed at strengthening rural communities, preserving the population's cultural values and raising its standard of living. It is being carried out in all Cuba's mountain areas, which make up 18 percent of national territory. Its results are notable in reforestation and the increase of coffee and cacao plantations. In recent years the process of migration has been reversed in almost all the country's mountain areas.

The development achieved by Cuban society is reflected by the high degree of equality and collective participation. Diverse foreign scholars have even come to very illustrative conclusions through independent research: growth of the per capita gross domestic product has been calculated at 3.1 percent annually from 1960 to 1985; of the country's total population, the 40 percent with the lowest income garner 26 percent of the total income; and the Gini coefficient for income distribution — an internationally recognized statistical formula for measuring equity — was 0.22 in 1986. This places Cuba among the most equitable countries in the world in this respect.

Cuba's equality is also guaranteed by collective access without distinction to the basic social services that determine the level and quality of life. This is perfectly measurable through the basic social indicators. In this sense, some may be surprised that Cuba, with a per capita GNP some 10 times less than the seven most industrialized countries, has achieved in the last 30 years health and education indicators similar and in some cases higher than those seven most industrialized countries. For example:

• the life expectancy rate of over 75 years is equal to that of those countries;

• the infant mortality rate for 1991 of 10.7 per 1000 live births is slightly higher than in those countries but close to those of Italy and the United States;

• today in Cuba there are more doctors per inhabitant and more primary teachers per student than in those countries as a whole;

• the number of births attended by health personnel is the same;

• the percentage of children immunized against the principal diseases is higher in Cuba;

• elementary and secondary school attendance is similar and the number of years of obligatory education is the same.

If comparisons with the richest countries of the world is not enough to convince someone of the equitable nature of Cuban society, it can also be seen in the variation of these indicators in the different regions of the country. Looking at the differences in the principal social indicators between national figures and provincial figures, it is clear that the variation between maximums and minimums for each of the aforementioned indicators is generally small, which means that national averages do not cover up large regional differences. Rarely do the maximum indices, which reveal the best instance of the indicator, appear in the capital. On the contrary, they often appear in territories which before the revolutionary process were among the most underdeveloped parts of the country.

Cuba is now facing the most difficult challenge in its history — it is well-known that the changes which took place in the former socialist countries of Eastern Europe and the former Soviet Union have had a major impact on the Cuban economy. About 85 percent of Cuba's trade was with those countries, and for that reason Cuba at this moment must withstand, in addition to the stepped-up blockade imposed for over 30 years by the United States, the effects of a second blockade provoked by these international changes.

In September 1990 the so-called special period in peacetime was begun. This is a period of readjustment given these new circumstances, requiring maximum economizing and austerity in economic and social policies, along with many creative initiatives, a large number of which have come directly from the people. Many of the steps taken as a result of the special period fit in with the strategic lines prepared by the Revolution. Some of them have helped accelerate the policies put into effect by the country in defense of the environment. An example of these are the measures undertaken as a result of the reduction of imported oil.

The most notable aspect is that we have been able to face the necessary reduction of electricity consumption with formulas that guarantee social security and popular participation, with significant ecological benefits. In order to cut household electricity consumption, we did not raise the price, which would have most seriously affected those with the lowest incomes, but established maximum consumption levels, with variations in accordance with the average amounts ordinarily consumed. Households were aware of this information and could plan the necessary consumption reductions.

To make cuts in transportation usage, a solution was introduced which is innovative because of its mass scale: the use of bicycles. Hundreds of thousands of bicycles were imported, several factories were modified to manufacture bicycles and almost half a million bicycles have been distributed to workers and students. The proliferation of cyclists of all ages is perfectly compatible with the policies promoted for several years to guarantee health for all, including exercise programs for senior citizens. In this way, the current shortages of fuel, although they negatively affect daily life, also have a positive effect on the environment.

Other examples of this kind which imply collective solutions — and which are ecologically valuable — are the intensified use of herbal medicine, the promotion of local fruit and vegetable gardens (even in residential areas in yards and terraces), the gradual utilization of animal traction in agriculture, the development of composting, and much more.

In finding alternative solutions to the difficulties of the special period, the country has the possibility of utilizing one of its most important achievements: the people's scientific and technical skills. The results of the priority given to such training are now significant. This is expressed in an educational level which translates into major advances in scientific research, with immediate applications in production which do not threaten the environment.

During the special period it has also been necessary to find alternative solutions in agricultural production, given the significant reduction in imports of chemical fertilizers and pesticides and livestock feed. Some of the results of the scientific research carried out in the last few years are being quickly put into practice. Among those which are notable for their ecological value and their level of generalization are the use of biofertilizers such as azotobacter, ryzobium and micorrhiza; the development of biological controls of blights and diseases, especially in the Centers for the Reproduction of Entomophagous Organisms and Entomopathogens, a broad network which has emerged in a short period of time; the quest for solutions to animal feed, such as the application of the rational pasturing system based on pasture rotation and natural fertilization by the cattle, the development of animal feed from sugarcane and by-products of the sugar industry; and other innovative solutions applied with singular speed, as soon as their viability and suitability are confirmed.

In the case of the sugar industry, the country's main economic branch, there has been a notable advance in waste treatment and its use not only on animal feed but in other spheres such as obtaining new sources of energy, fertilizer spray and paper manufacture.

The intensification of these solutions is only possible through the accumulation of knowledge. The ecological convergence is not accidental either, but rather responds to a defined development strategy harmonizing care for the environment with economic and social progress.

A plan of action

Cuba's scientific research potential and skilled human resources allow it to translate its willingness to cooperate with the United Nations and other international governmental and nongovernmental organizations in programs of environmental and social assistance to Third World countries. A first proposal, therefore, among the many that could be made, is to provide technical personnel in areas such as health care, education, agriculture and environmental protection, and to offer all the cooperation possible in the sphere of scientific research, in which Cuba has made considerable breakthroughs.

There is no doubt that the biological diversity agreement presented at this conference, and the steps that it will lead to are a worthy effort to protect both the present and future wealth encompassed in biological diversity and the safe and rational use of the results of biotechnological research. It nevertheless seems beyond doubt that in the present circumstances Third World countries need to develop and deepen their cooperation in these spheres. That is why Cuba has thought it pertinent to create a permanent forum of the South for the protection and preservation of biological diversity and for access to biotechnological development.

The aim of this proposal would be to create a mechanism for the consultation and conciliation of ideas and projects, stripped of red tape, that would give Third World countries the opportunity to continue debating these issues that are of such vital importance to them. It would also enable them to adopt a common position in preparation for the members' conference that would take place once the treaty is ratified. This permanent forum could focus its analysis on, among others, the following questions:

• the establishment of a common system for the legal protection of genetic resources which would include appropriate compensation procedures for access to these resources;

• the implimentation of common mechanisms capable of facilitating access to developed biotechnology based on the genetic resources contributed;

• the creation of advisory facilities in Third World countries that have shown major advances in the scientific sphere, including technical training of personnel and the exchange of specialists from the various branches of science;

• the formation of common approaches to the defense of the indigenous people's identity — lifestyles, culture, language, traditions — and their age-old knowledge of the vital link between humans and the environment;

• the elaboration of common defense mechanisms against the introduction of potentially dangerous modified organisms into the environment;

• the creation of facilities for the legal protection of natural resources and of the results of research carried out in Third World countries.

Alongside this consultation system, the possibility of establishing a center for the conservation of biological diversity in the countries of the South could be considered. All the countries that have signed the biological diversity convention at this conference would participate and the headquarters should be located in a country possessing a rich biological diversity. Brazil, which has been an efficient and appropriate host for this meeting, would without a doubt be a good choice. The main objective of this center would be the in situ preservation of diverse ecosystems and the ex situ conservation of tropical genetic resources.

In the 20 years that have gone by since the first meeting on the environment in Stockholm, the world population grew by 1.6 billion inhabitants, 80 percent of these in the Third World; extreme poverty extended to more than one billion human beings; hunger reached unprecedented proportions; and infections and deficiency diseases affected hundreds of millions of people. During this period, almost 250 million children under the age of five and some 10 million women died of cases related to childbirth in the Third World. During those years, the world lost 480 billion metric tons of agricultural topsoil; 300 million hectares of forest land were razed; deserts spread by more than 120 million hectares; the per capita production of food stayed constant or decreased in the Third World; immeasurable water sources were either polluted or dried up; and tens of thousands of animal and plant species became extinct.

Today it is being proposed that a global system of environmental security be established that would have the agreement and participation of all nations. There has been a lot of talk about global security in political and military terms. This quest has led to gigantic military forces. Millions of minds and the efforts of international scientific research have been sacrificed to those interests. The essential resources needed to counter social and economic disaster in the underdeveloped world, with foreseeable political, social and ecological consequences, have been squandered. In the present circumstances, if a true climate of international peace and detente were created, global security would depend on the protection of nature, which is the responsibility of all, and on the effective solution of underdevelopment and poverty in the Third World.

Humanity can still stop and reverse the destruction of the environment. It nevertheless seems appropriate to ask how much time it has to do so. If present trends continue, in 40 years the earth's population will have doubled, the climate will have suffered deep and irreversible changes, the tropical rain forests will have practically disappeared; immense deserts, sterile and degraded lands will have replaced a large part of the lands that are now used for crops and livestock raising; clean water will be very hard or impossible to find in entire regions; and hunger will spread uncontrollably and irremediably.

There are some who minimize the importance of these problems for political and economic reasons. The indifferent attitude adopted years ago by those who wanted to defend their privileged position derived from opulence, waste and consumerism has led humanity to its present crossroads. Humanity now faces an uncertain future in which the rich and developed peoples will be united with and on the same footing as the poor of the earth in facing the threat to their existence and their lack of future prospects — all for having failed to take concrete and effective measures in time.

Without a doubt, unequivocal political will is needed to solve this crisis. Abundant financial resources, which exist and can be obtained in the present international conditions, are also needed. In the last 20 years the world has squandered over $13 trillion in military spending. Even in 1991, with the cold war and the danger of a confrontation between superpowers in the past, military spending was almost a trillion dollars. Those are the resources to finance these programs.

This conference's success will be measured in the associations that flow from it. We represent humanity, and that moral duty, that political obligation, that exceptional and historical responsibility demands concrete decisions and measures and a commitment that can no longer be put off.

Can Cuba Survive?

An interview with Fidel Castro

In a frank exchange with Mexican journalist Beatriz Pagés, Cuban leader Fidel Castro confronts the realities of Cuba in a "new world order." In this book length interview he considers the issues facing his own country.

What is the situation in Cuba since the collapse of the socialist countries of Europe? Are socialism and democracy compatible? What chance is there of Latin American integration? How should Latin America respond to the 500th anniversary of Spanish colonization? What real power does Fidel Castro have in Cuba? Why is Cuba an obsession for the United States? How does Fidel Castro see his personal role in Cuba and his place in history?

Lastly, Cuban President Fidel Castro accepts the challenge to answer the most controversial question: Can Cuba survive?

105 pages, ISBN paper 1-875284-58-3

Island in the storm

The Cuban Communist Party's Fourth Congress
Edited by Gail Reed

Island in the Storm describes Cuba's strategy for survival, as it emerged from the most critical meeting in the revolution's history. This volume contains the unedited texts of all Congress resolutions, Fidel Castro's first detailed disclosure of the state of the Cuban economy, biographies of the new Cuban leadership, plus as-yet unpublished excerpts from Congress discussions and conversations with delegates.

Introductory essays on each issue tackled by the assembly offer valuable data and perspective on major policy shifts and the nuances of Congress debate.

Island in the Storm editor is Gail Reed, the only foreign journalist to attend the Fourth Congress of the Cuban Communist Party. She has reported from inside Cuba for the last decade, both for the Cuban national press and US radio and print media.

Published in association with the Center for Cuban Studies.

200 pages, ISBN paper 1-875284-48-6

The Cuban Revolution and the United States

A Chronological History
by Jane Franklin

An invaluable resource for scholars, teachers, journalists, legislators, and anyone interested in international relations, this volume offers an unprecedented vision of Cuban-US relations. Cuba watchers will wonder how they got along without it.

Based on exceptionally wide research, this history provides a day by day, year by year report of developments involving Cuba and the United States from January 1, 1959, through 1990. An introductory section, starting with the arrival of Christopher Columbus in the Caribbean, chronicles the events that led to the triumph of the revolution in Cuba in 1959.

Indispensable as a reference guide, *The Cuban Revolution and the United States* is also an eye-opening narrative, interrelating major crises with seemingly minor or secret episodes.

Published in association with the Center for Cuban Studies.

276 pages, ISBN paper 1-875284-26-5/cloth 1-875284-42-7